If you want to change the world . . .

MAKE YOUR BED

ADMIRAL
WILLIAM H. McRAVEN
(*U.S. Navy Retired*)

MAKE YOUR BED

LITTLE THINGS THAT CAN
CHANGE YOUR LIFE
...AND MAYBE THE WORLD

MICHAEL JOSEPH
an imprint of
PENGUIN BOOKS

MICHAEL JOSEPH

UK | USA | Canada | Ireland | Australia
India | New Zealand | South Africa

Michael Joseph is part of the Penguin Random House group of companies
whose addresses can be found at global.penguinrandomhouse.com.

Penguin
Random House
UK

First published in the United States of America by Grand Central
Publishing, a division of Hachette Book Group, Inc. 2017
First published in Great Britain by Michael Joseph 2017

004

Print book interior design by Jason Heuer

Printed in Great Britain by Clays Ltd, St Ives plc

A CIP catalogue record for this book is available from the British Library

ISBN: 978–0–718–18886–3

www.greenpenguin.co.uk

MIX
Paper from
responsible sources
FSC® C018179

Penguin Random House is committed to a
sustainable future for our business, our readers
and our planet. This book is made from Forest
Stewardship Council® certified paper.

To my three children: Bill, John, and Kelly. No father could be prouder of his kids than I am of you. Every moment in my life has been made better because you are in the world. And to my wife, Georgeann, my best friend, who made all of my dreams possible. Where would I be without you?

CONTENTS

PREFACE

On May 17, 2014, I was honored to give the commencement speech for the graduating class from the University of Texas at Austin. Even though the university was my alma mater, I was concerned that a military officer, whose career had been defined by war, might not find a welcoming audience among college students. But to my great surprise, the graduating class embraced the speech. The ten lessons I learned from Navy SEAL training, which were the basis for my remarks, seemed to have a universal appeal. They were simple lessons that deal with overcoming the trials of SEAL training, but the ten lessons were equally important in dealing with the challenges of life—no matter who you are. Over the past three years, I have been stopped on the street by great folks telling me their own stories: How they didn't back down from the sharks, how they didn't ring the bell, or how making their bed every morning helped them through tough times. They all wanted to know more about how the ten lessons shaped my life and about the people who inspired me during my career. This small book is an attempt to do so. Each chapter gives a little more context to the individual lessons and also adds a short story about some of the people who inspired me with their discipline, their perseverance, their honor, and their courage. I hope you enjoy the book!

MAKE YOUR BED

CHAPTER ONE

Start Your Day with a Task Completed

If you want to change the world . . .

start off by making your bed.

The barracks at basic SEAL training is a nondescript three-story building located on the beach at Coronado, California, just one hundred yards from the Pacific Ocean. There is no air-conditioning in the building, and at night, with the windows open, you can hear the tide roll in and the surf pounding against the sand.

Rooms in the barracks are spartan. In the officers' room, where I berthed with three other classmates, there were four beds, a closet to hang your uniforms, and nothing else. Those mornings that I stayed in the barracks I would roll out of my Navy "rack" and immediately begin the process of making my bed. It was the first task of the day. A day that I knew would be filled with uniform inspections, long swims, longer runs, obstacle courses, and constant harassment from the SEAL instructors.

"Attention!" shouted the class leader, Lieutenant Junior Grade Dan'l Steward, as the instructor entered the room. Standing at the foot of the bed, I snapped my heels together and stood up straight as a chief petty officer approached my position. The instructor, stern and expressionless, began the inspection by checking the starch in my green uniform hat to ensure the eight-sided "cover" was crisp and correctly blocked. Moving from top to bottom, his eyes looked over every inch of my uniform. Were the creases in the blouse and trousers aligned? Was the brass on the belt shined to a mirrorlike radiance? Were my boots polished bright enough so he could see his fingers in their reflection? Satisfied that I met the high standards expected of a SEAL trainee, he moved to inspect the bed.

The bed was as simple as the room, nothing but a steel frame and a single mattress. A bottom sheet covered the mattress, and over that was a top sheet. A gray wool blanket tucked tightly under the mattress provided warmth from the cool San Diego evenings.

A second blanket was expertly folded into a rectangle at the foot of the bed. A single pillow, made by the Lighthouse for the Blind, was centered at the top of the bed and intersected at a ninety-degree angle with the blanket at the bottom. This was the standard. Any deviation from this exacting requirement would be cause for me to "hit the surf" and then roll around on the beach until I was covered head to toe with wet sand—referred to as a "sugar cookie."

Standing motionless, I could see the instructor out of the corner of my eye. He wearily looked at my bed. Bending over, he checked the hospital corners and then surveyed the blanket and the pillow to ensure they were correctly aligned. Then, reaching into his pocket, he pulled out a quarter and flipped it into the air several times to ensure I knew the final test of the bed was coming. With one final flip the quarter flew high into the air and came down on the mattress with a light bounce. It jumped several inches off the bed, high enough for the instructor to catch it in his hand.

Swinging around to face me, the instructor looked me in the eye and nodded. He never said a word. Making my bed correctly was not going to be an opportunity for praise. It was expected of me. It was my first task of the day, and doing it right was important. It demonstrated my discipline. It showed my attention to detail, and at the end of the day it would be a reminder that I had done something well, something to be proud of, no matter how small the task.

Throughout my life in the Navy, making my bed was the one constant that I could count on every day. As a young SEAL ensign aboard the USS *Grayback*, a special operation submarine, I was berthed in sick bay, where the beds were stacked four high. The salty old doctor who ran sick bay insisted that I make my rack every morning. He often remarked that if the beds were not made and the room was not clean, how could the sailors expect the best medical care? As I later found out, this sentiment of cleanliness and order applied to every aspect of military life.

Thirty years later, the Twin Towers came down in New York City. The Pentagon was struck, and brave Americans died in an airplane over Pennsylvania.

At the time of the attacks, I was recuperating in my home from a serious parachute accident. A hospital bed had been wheeled into my government quarters, and I spent most of the day lying on my back, trying to recover. I wanted out of that bed more than anything else. Like every SEAL I longed to be with my fellow warriors in the fight.

When I was finally well enough to lift myself unaided from the bed, the first thing I did was pull the sheets up tight, adjust the pillow, and make sure the hospital bed looked presentable to all those who entered my home. It was my way of showing that I had conquered the injury and was moving forward with my life.

Within four weeks of 9/11, I was transferred to the White House, where I spent the next two years in the newly formed Office of Combatting

Terrorism. By October 2003, I was in Iraq at our makeshift headquarters on the Baghdad airfield. For the first few months we slept on Army cots. Nevertheless, I would wake every morning, roll up my sleeping bag, place the pillow at the head of the cot, and get ready for the day.

In December 2003, U.S. forces captured Saddam Hussein. He was held in confinement during which time we kept him in a small room. He also slept on an Army cot, but with the luxury of sheets and a blanket. Once a day I would visit Saddam to ensure my soldiers were properly caring for him. I noticed, with some sense of amusement, that Saddam did not make his bed. The covers were always crumpled at the foot of his cot and he rarely seemed inclined to straighten them.

During the ensuing ten years, I had the honor of working with some of the finest men and women this nation has ever produced—from generals to privates, from admirals to seamen recruits, from ambassadors to clerk typists. The Americans who deployed overseas in support of the war effort came willingly, sacrificing much to protect this great nation.

They all understood that life is hard and that sometimes there is little you can do to affect the outcome of your day. In battle soldiers die, families grieve, your days are long and filled with anxious moments. You search for something that can give you solace, that can motivate you to begin your day, that can be a sense of pride in an oftentimes ugly world. But it is not just combat. It is daily life that needs this same sense of structure. Nothing can replace the strength and comfort of one's faith, but sometimes the simple act of making your bed can give you the lift you need to start your day and provide you the satisfaction to end it right.

If you want to change your life and maybe the world—start off by making your bed!

CHAPTER TWO

You Can't Go It Alone

If you want to change the world . . .

find someone to help you paddle.

I learned early on in SEAL training the value of teamwork, the need to rely on someone else to help you through the difficult tasks. For those of us who were "tadpoles" hoping to become Navy frogmen, a ten-foot rubber raft was used to teach us this vital lesson.

Everywhere we went during the first phase of SEAL training we were required to carry the raft. We placed it on our heads as we ran from the barracks, across the highway, to the chow hall. We carried it in a low-slung position as we ran up and down the Coronado sand dunes. We paddled the boat endlessly from north to south along the coastline and through the pounding surf, seven men, all working together to get the rubber boat to its final destination.

But we learned something else on our journey

with the raft. Occasionally, one of the boat crew members was sick or injured, unable to give it 100 percent. I often found myself exhausted from the training day, or down with a cold or the flu. On those days, the other members picked up the slack. They paddled harder. They dug deeper. They gave me their rations for extra strength. And when the time came, later in training, I returned the favor. The small rubber boat made us realize that no man could make it through training alone. No SEAL could make it through combat alone and by extension you needed people in your life to help you through the difficult times.

———

Never was the need for help more apparent to me than twenty-five years later when I commanded all the SEALs on the West Coast.

I was the commodore of Naval Special Warfare Group ONE in Coronado. A Navy captain, I had by now spent the past several decades leading SEALs around the world. I was out for a routine parachute jump when things went terribly wrong.

We were in a C-130 Hercules aircraft climbing to twelve thousand feet preparing for the jump. Looking out the back of the aircraft, we could see a beautiful California day. Not a cloud in the sky. The Pacific Ocean was calm, and from this altitude you could see the border of Mexico just a few miles away.

The jumpmaster yelled to "stand by." Now on the edge of the ramp, I could see straight down to the ground. The jumpmaster looked me in the eye, smiled, and shouted, "Go, go, go!" I dove out of the aircraft, arms fully extended and legs tucked slightly behind my back. The prop blast from the aircraft sent me tilting forward until my arms caught air and I leveled out.

I quickly checked my altimeter, made sure I wasn't spinning, and then looked around me to ensure no jumper was too close to me. Twenty seconds later I had fallen to the pull altitude of 5,500 feet.

Suddenly, I looked below me and another

jumper had slid beneath me, intersecting my path to the ground. He pulled his rip cord, and I could see the pilot chute deploying the main parachute from his backpack. Immediately, I thrust my arms to my side, forcing my head to the ground in an attempt to get away from the blossoming chute. It was too late.

The jumper's chute popped open in front of me like an air bag, hitting me at 120 miles an hour. I bounced off the main canopy and spun out of control, barely conscious from the impact. For seconds I spun head over heels, trying to get stable again. I couldn't see my altimeter and was unaware of how far I had fallen.

Instinctively, I reached for my rip cord and pulled. The pilot chute jettisoned from its small pouch in the back of the parachute but wrapped around my leg as I continued to tumble toward the ground. As I struggled to untangle myself the situation got worse. The main parachute partially deployed but in doing so twirled around my other leg.

Craning my neck toward the sky, I could see

my legs were bound by two sets of risers, the long nylon straps that connect the main parachute to the harness on my back. One riser had wrapped around one leg, the other riser around the other leg. The main parachute was fully out of the backpack but hung up somewhere on my body.

As I struggled to break free of the entanglement, suddenly I felt the canopy lift off my body and begin to open. Looking toward my legs, I knew what was coming next.

Within seconds, the canopy caught air. The two risers, one wrapped around each leg, suddenly and violently pulled apart, taking my legs with them. My pelvis separated instantly as the force of the opening ripped my lower torso. The thousand small muscles that connect the pelvis to the body were torn from their hinges.

My mouth dropped open and I let out a scream that could be heard in Mexico. Searing pain arched through my body, sending waves pulsating downward to my pelvis and upward to my head. Violent, muscular convulsions racked my upper torso, shooting more pain through my arms and legs. Now, like having an out-of-body experience, I became aware of my screaming and tried to control it, but the pain was too intense.

Still head down and falling too fast, I turned myself upright in the harness, relieving some of the pressure on my pelvis and back.

Fifteen hundred feet.

I had fallen over four thousand feet before the parachute deployed. The good news: I had a full canopy over my head. The bad news: I was broken apart by the impact of the opening.

I landed over two miles from the drop zone. Within a few minutes the drop zone crew and an ambulance arrived. I was taken to the trauma hospital in downtown San Diego. By the next day I was out of surgery. The accident had ripped my pelvis apart by almost five inches. The muscles in my stomach had become detached from the pelvic bone and the muscles in my back and legs were severely damaged from the opening shock. I had a large titanium plate screwed into my pelvis and a long scapular screw drilled into my backside for stability.

This seemed like the end of my career. To be an effective SEAL you had to be physically fit. My rehabilitation was going to take months, maybe years, and the Navy was required to conduct a medical evaluation to determine if I was fit for duty. I left the hospital seven days later but remained bedridden at my home for the next two months.

All my life I had the feeling I was invincible. I believed that my innate athletic abilities could get me out of most perilous situations. And, up to this point, I had been right. Many times during my career I had encountered life-threatening incidents: midair collisions in another parachute; uncontrolled descent in a minisub; nearly falling hundreds of feet off an oil rig; getting trapped beneath a sinking boat; demolition that exploded prematurely; and countless more—incidents where a split second decided the fate between living and dying. Each time I had somehow managed to make the right decision, and each time I was physically fit enough to overcome the challenge before me. Not this time.

Now, lying in bed, all I felt was self-pity. But that would not last for long. My wife, Georgeann, had been given nursing duties. She cleaned my wounds, gave me the required daily shots, and changed my bedpan. But most importantly, she reminded me of who I was. I had never given up on anything in my life and she assured me that I was not going to start now. She refused to let me feel sorry for myself. It was the kind of tough love that I needed, and as the days went by, I got better.

My friends came by the house, called constantly, and helped with whatever they could. My boss, Admiral Eric Olson, somehow found a way around the policy that required the Navy to conduct a medical evaluation of my ability to continue to serve as a SEAL. His support for me likely saved my career.

During my time in the SEAL Teams I had numerous setbacks, and in each case, someone came forward to help me: someone who had faith in my abilities; someone who saw potential in me where others might not; someone who risked their own reputation to advance my career. I have never forgotten those people and I know that anything I achieved in my life was a result of others who have helped me along the way.

None of us are immune from life's tragic moments. Like the small rubber boat we had in basic SEAL training, it takes a team of good people to get you to your destination in life. You cannot paddle the boat alone. Find someone to share your life with. Make as many friends as possible, and never forget that your success depends on others.

CHAPTER THREE

Only the Size of Your Heart Matters

If you want to change the world . . .

measure a person by the size
of their heart.

I ran to the beach with my black, rubber flippers tucked underneath my right arm and my mask in my left hand. Coming to parade rest, I anchored the flippers in the soft sand, leaning them against each other to form a teepee. Standing to my right and left were other students. Dressed in green tee shirts, khaki swim trunks, neoprene booties, and a small life jacket, we were preparing for our morning two-mile swim.

The life jacket was a small, rubberized bladder that inflated only when you pulled the handle. Among the students, it was considered shameful if you had to use your life jacket. Still, the SEAL instructors were required to inspect every life jacket before each swim. This inspection also gave the instructors an opportunity for more harassment.

The surf off Coronado that day was about eight

feet high. The waves were coming in lines of three, plunging with a roaring sound that made each student's heart beat a bit faster. As the instructor slowly moved down the line he came to the man directly to my right. The student, a seaman recruit and brand-new to the Navy, was about five foot four in height. The SEAL instructor, a highly decorated Vietnam vet, was well above six foot two and towered over the smaller man.

After inspecting the student's life jacket, the instructor looked over his left shoulder toward the pounding surf and then reached down and grabbed the student's flippers. Holding them close to the young sailor's face, he said quietly, "Do you really want to be a frogman?"

The sailor stood up straight, with a look of defiance in his eyes. "Yes, instructor, I do!" he shouted.

"You're a tiny little man," the instructor said, waving the flippers in his face. "Those waves out there could break you in half." He paused and glanced toward the ocean. "You should think about quitting now before you get hurt."

Even out of the corner of my eye I could see the student's jaw begin to tighten.

"I won't quit!" the sailor replied, drawing out each word. Then the instructor leaned in and whispered something in the student's ear. I couldn't make out the words over the breaking waves.

After all the trainees were inspected the instructors ordered us into the water, and we began our swim. An hour later, I crawled out of the surf zone, and standing on the beach was the young seaman recruit. He had finished the swim near the head of the class. Later that day, I pulled him aside and asked what the instructor had whispered to him. He smiled and said proudly, "Prove me wrong!"

SEAL training was always about proving something. Proving that size didn't matter. Proving that the color of your skin wasn't important. Proving that money didn't make you better. Proving that

determination and grit were always more important than talent. I was fortunate to learn that lesson
a year before training began.

———

As I boarded the city bus in downtown San Diego I
was excited about the prospect of visiting the basic
SEAL training facility across the bay in Coronado. I
was a first-class midshipman attending my summer
cruise as part of the Naval Reserve Officers Training
Corp (ROTC) program. As a first-class midshipman
I was between my junior and senior years in college,
and if all went well, I hoped to be commissioned the
following summer and head off to SEAL training.
It was the middle of the week and I had received
permission from my ROTC instructor to deviate
from the planned training aboard one of the ships in
port and make my way to Coronado.

I got off the bus outside the famed Hotel del
Coronado and walked about a mile down the road
to the beach side of the Naval Amphibious Base. I

passed by several Korean War–vintage buildings that housed Underwater Demolition Teams Eleven and Twelve. Outside the one-story rambling brick building was a large wooden sign depicting Freddy the Frog, a large green web-footed amphibian carrying a stick of TNT and smoking a cigar. This was the home of the West Coast frogmen, those intrepid mask-and-fin warriors whose military ancestors had cleared the beaches of Iwo Jima, Tarawa, Guam, and Inchon. My heart began to beat a little faster. This was exactly where I wanted to be in a year.

As I passed the Underwater Demolition Teams the next building belonged to SEAL Team One, at the time a new breed of jungle fighters who had earned their reputation in Vietnam as some of the toughest men in the military. Another large wooden sign showed Sammy the Seal, a dagger in one hand and a dark cloak wrapped around his shoulders. As I would later learn, the frogmen and the SEALs were one and the same. All the men were graduates of SEAL training, all frogmen at heart.

Finally, I approached the last government building on the beach side of the naval base. On the outer facade of the building it read, BASIC UNDERWATER DEMOLITION SEAL TRAINING. Standing outside the main entrance were two SEAL instructors surrounded by some young high school sea cadets. The two SEALs towered over the high school students. Senior Chief Petty Officer Dick Ray stood six foot three with broad shoulders, a thin waist, a deep tan, and a dark pencil-thin mustache. He was everything I expected a SEAL to look like. Standing next to him was Chief Petty Officer Gene Wence. Well over six feet, Wence was built like a linebacker, with imposing biceps and a steely-eyed glare that cautioned everyone not to get too close.

The sea cadets were ushered into the building. With some trepidation, I followed them and stopped at the front desk. I told the young sailor manning the desk my story. I was a midshipman from the University of Texas and hoped to talk with someone about SEAL training. The sailor left his desk momentarily, returning to inform me that the first phase officer, Lieutenant Doug Huth, would be glad to talk with me in a few minutes.

As I waited to be called into Lieutenant Huth's office I slowly walked up and down the hall, looking at the pictures that adorned the walls. They were photos of SEALs in Vietnam, guys rising out of the waist-deep mud along the Mekong Delta. Pictures of camouflaged SEAL platoons returning from a night mission. Men loaded with automatic weapons and bandoliers of ammunition boarding a Swift boat heading into the jungle.

Down the long hall I saw another man looking at the photos. A civilian by his attire, he was slightly built, almost frail, and a mop of dark hair hung Beatle-like over his ears. He seemed to be staring in awe at the incredible warriors whose actions were portrayed in the photos. In my mind, I wondered if he thought he had what it took to be a Navy SEAL. Looking at those pictures, did he really think he was tough enough to endure the training? Did he think his small frame could carry a heavy rucksack and a thousand rounds of ammunition? Hadn't he seen the two SEAL instructors who were just at the front door? Massive men who clearly had the right stuff? I felt a pang of sorrow that someone had misled this fellow, maybe encouraged him to leave his comfortable life as a civilian and try SEAL training.

A few minutes later, the sailor from the front desk calmly walked down the corridor and escorted me to Lieutenant Huth's office. Doug Huth was also a recruiting poster for the SEALs; tall, muscular, with brown, wavy hair, he looked very sharp in his Navy khaki uniform.

I sat in a chair across from Huth's desk, and we talked about SEAL training and the demands of the program. Huth told me about his experience in Vietnam and what life would be like in the Teams if I graduated from SEAL training. Out of the corner of my eye, I could see the thin man in civilian clothes as he continued to gaze at the photos on the wall. Like me, he must have been waiting to see

Lieutenant Huth in hopes of learning more about SEAL training. It made me feel good about myself knowing that I was clearly stronger and more prepared than another man who thought he could survive the rigors of being a SEAL.

In the middle of our conversation, Lieutenant Huth suddenly stopped talking, looked up from his desk, and yelled to the man in the hall. I stood up as Huth motioned the thin man to come into his office. "Bill, this is Tommy Norris," he said, giving the thin man a big bear hug. "Tommy was the last SEAL Medal of Honor recipient from Vietnam," Huth added. Norris smiled, somewhat embarrassed by the introduction. I smiled back, shook his hand, and laughed at myself. This seemingly frail, mop-haired man who I doubted could make it through training was Lieutenant Tom Norris. Tom Norris, who had served in Vietnam, had on successive nights gone deep behind enemy lines to rescue two downed airmen. This was Tom Norris who, on another mission, was shot in the face by North Vietnamese forces and left for dead only to be rescued by Petty Officer Mike Thornton, who would later receive the Medal of Honor for those actions. This was Tom Norris, who battled back from his injury to be accepted into the FBI's first Hostage Rescue Team. This quiet, reserved, humble man was one of the toughest SEALs in the long history of the Teams.

In 1969, Tommy Norris was almost booted out of SEAL training. They said he was too small, too thin, and not strong enough. But much like the young sailor in my class, Norris proved them all wrong and once again showed that it's not the size of your flippers that count, just the size of your heart.

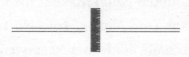

CHAPTER FOUR

Life's Not Fair—Drive On!

If you want to change the world . . .

get over being a sugar cookie
and keep moving forward.

I ran to the top of the sand dune and without hesitation sprinted down the other side, heading full speed toward the Pacific Ocean. Fully clothed in my green utilities, short-billed hat, and combat boots, I dove headfirst into the waves as they pounded the beach off Coronado, California.

Emerging soaking wet from the water, I saw the SEAL instructor standing on the dune. With his arms folded and a piercing glare that cut through the morning haze, I heard him yell, "You know what to do, Mr. Mac!"

Indeed I did.

With feigned enthusiasm, I screamed a hearty "hooyah" at the top of my lungs and fell facedown into the soft sand, rolling from side to side to ensure that no part of my uniform was left uncovered. Then, for good measure, I sat up, reached deep into the ground, and tossed sand into the air to guarantee it found its way into every crevice in my body.

Somewhere during the morning's physical training I had "committed a violation of the SEAL training rules." My punishment was to jump into the surf zone, roll around in the sand, and make myself a "sugar cookie."

In all of SEAL training there was nothing more uncomfortable than being a sugar cookie. There were a lot of things more painful and more exhausting, but being a sugar cookie tested your patience and your determination. Not just because you spent the rest of the day with sand down your neck, under your arms, and between your legs, but because the act of becoming a sugar cookie was completely indiscriminate. There was no rhyme or reason. You became a sugar cookie at the whim of the instructor.

To many of the SEAL trainees this was hard to accept. Those that strived to be the very best expected that they would be rewarded for their stellar performance. Sometimes they were and, then again, sometimes they were not. Sometimes the only thing they got for all their effort was wet and sandy.

Feeling like I was sufficiently coated with sand, I ran to the instructor, yelled "hooyah" again, and came to attention. Looking me over to see if I met his standard of excellence in sugar cookies was Lieutenant Phillip L. Martin, known to his friends as Moki. I, however, was not on a first-name basis with Lieutenant Martin.

Moki Martin was the quintessential frogman. Born and raised in Hawaii, he was everything I strived to be as a SEAL officer. An experienced Vietnam veteran, he was expert with every weapon in the SEAL inventory. He was one of the finest skydivers in the Teams, and being a native Hawaiian, he was so skilled in the water that there were few, if any, who could match him.

"Mr. Mac, do you have any idea why you are a sugar cookie this morning?" Martin said in a very calm but questioning manner.

"No, Instructor Martin," I dutifully responded.

"Because, Mr. Mac, life isn't fair and the sooner you learn that the better off you will be."

A year later, Lieutenant Martin and I were on a first-name basis. I had completed basic SEAL training, and he had been reassigned from the training center to Underwater Demolition Team Eleven in Coronado.

The more I got to know Moki, the deeper my respect grew for him. In addition to being a superb SEAL operator, Moki was also a phenomenal athlete. In the early 1980s, he was on the leading edge of the triathlon craze. He had a beautiful freestyle stroke in the open ocean. His calves and thighs were strong and moved him effortlessly on the long runs, but his real advantage was the bicycle. He and the bike were made for each other.

Every morning he would mount the bike and go for a thirty-mile ride up and down the Coronado Silver Strand. There was a flat stretch of paved bike path that paralleled the Pacific Ocean. It ran from the city of Coronado to the city of Imperial Beach. With the ocean on one side and the bay on the other, it was one of the most beautiful sections of beach in California.

Early one Saturday morning, Moki was out on a training ride along the Silver Strand. Head down, pedaling fast, he never saw the oncoming bicycle. At roughly twenty-five miles an hour the two bikes collided head-on. The bikes crumpled from the impact, slamming the riders together, leaving both men facedown on the asphalt path. The first rider rolled over, dusted himself off, and struggled to his feet. He was banged up but otherwise fine.

Moki remained facedown, unable to move. The paramedics arrived within minutes, stabilized Moki, and transported him to the hospital. Initially there was hope that the paralysis was temporary, but as the days, months, and years passed, Moki never regained the use of his legs. The crash left him paralyzed from the waist down with limited movement in his arms.

For the past thirty-five years, Moki has been in a wheelchair. In all those years I never once heard him complain about his misfortune in life. Never once did I hear him ask, "Why me?" Never once did he display an ounce of pity for himself.

In fact, after his accident, Moki went on to be an accomplished painter. He fathered a beautiful young girl. He founded and continues to oversee the Super Frog Triathlon that is held every year in Coronado.

It is easy to blame your lot in life on some outside force, to stop trying because you believe fate is against you. It is easy to think that where you were raised, how your parents treated you, or what school you went to is all that determines your future. Nothing could be further from the truth. The common people and the great men and women are all defined by how they deal with life's unfairness: Helen Keller, Nelson Mandela, Stephen Hawking, Malala Yousafzai, and—Moki Martin.

Sometimes no matter how hard you try, no matter how good you are, you still end up as a sugar cookie. Don't complain. Don't blame it on your misfortune. Stand tall, look to the future, and drive on!

CHAPTER FIVE

Failure Can Make You Stronger

If you want to change the world . . .

don't be afraid of The Circus.

The waves off Coronado Island were choppy, the small whitecaps slapping us in the face as we sidestroked back toward the beach. As usual, my swim buddy and I were struggling to keep up with the rest of the SEAL training class. The instructors on the safety boat were yelling for us to pick up the pace, but it seemed like the harder we swam the farther we fell behind.

My swim buddy that day was Ensign Marc Thomas. Like me, Marc had received his commission through the Reserve Officers Training Corps (ROTC). He was a graduate of the Virginia Military Institute and one of the best long-distance runners in the class.

In SEAL training your swim buddy was the person you relied on to have your back. It was your swim buddy who you were physically tied to on the underwater dives. It was your swim buddy who you were partnered with on the long swims. Your swim buddy helped you study, kept you motivated, and became your closest ally throughout training. And, as swim buddies, if one of you failed an event, both of you suffered the consequences. It was the instructors' way of reinforcing the importance of teamwork.

As we finished the swim and crossed onto the beach, a SEAL instructor was waiting for us.

"Drop down!" the instructor yelled. This was the command to fall into the push-up position: back straight, arms fully extended, and head up.

"You two call yourselves officers?" There was no point in answering. We both knew he would continue.

"Officers in the SEAL Teams lead the way. They don't come in last on the swims. They don't embarrass their class."

The instructor moved around us, kicking sand in our faces as he circled.

"I don't think you gentlemen are going to make it. I don't think you have what it takes to be SEAL officers."

Pulling a small black notebook from his back

pocket, he looked at us with disgust and jotted something in the book. "You two just made The Circus list." He shook his head. "You'll be lucky if you survive another week."

The Circus. It was the last thing either Marc or I wanted. The Circus was held every afternoon at the end of training. The Circus was another two hours of additional calisthenics, combined with nonstop harassment by SEAL combat veterans who wanted only the strong to survive training. If you failed to meet the standard on any event that day—calisthenics, the obstacle course, the timed runs, or the swims—your name was on the list. In the eyes of the instructors, you were a failure.

What made The Circus so feared by the students was not just the additional pain but also the knowledge that the day after The Circus you would be exhausted from the extra workout and so fatigued that you would fail to meet the standards again. Another Circus would follow, then another and another. It was a death spiral, a cycle of failure that caused many students to quit training.

As the rest of the students completed the day's events, Marc and I, along with several others, assembled on the asphalt grinder to begin another long session of calisthenics.

Because we had come in last on the swim, the instructors had tailored The Circus just for us that day. Flutter kicks. Lots and lots of flutter kicks. The flutter kicks were designed to strengthen your abdominals and thighs so you could power your way through the long open ocean swims. They were also designed to break you.

The flutter kick exercise called for you to lie on your back, with legs extended directly in front of you, and your hands behind your head. As the instructor counted repetitions, you alternated moving your legs up and down in a kicking motion. At no time during the exercise were you allowed to bend your knees. Bending your knees was considered weakness among frogmen.

The Circus was punishing. Hundreds of flutter kicks as well as push-ups, pull-ups, sit-ups, and eight-count body builders. By the time the sun went down Marc and I could barely move. Failure had a price.

The next day brought more calisthenics, another run, another obstacle course, another swim, and unfortunately another Circus. More sit-ups, more push-ups, and a lot more flutter kicks. But as The Circuses continued a funny thing happened. Our swims got better, and Marc and I began to move up in the pack.

The Circus, which had started as a punishment for failure, was making us stronger, faster, and more confident in the water. While other students quit, unable to handle the occasional failure and the pain it brought, Marc and I were determined not to allow The Circus to beat us.

As training was coming to an end, there was one final open ocean swim, a five-miler off the coast of San Clemente Island. Completing it in the allowable time was essential to graduating from SEAL training.

The water was bitterly cold as we jumped off the pier and into the ocean. Fifteen swim pairs entered the water and began the long trek out of the small bay, around the peninsula, and over the kelp beds. After about two hours, the swim pairs were so spread out you couldn't tell where you were in the pack. Four hours into the swim, numb, exhausted, and on the verge of hypothermia, Marc Thomas and I crossed the beach. There waiting at the surf's edge was the instructor.

"Drop down," he yelled.

My hands and feet were so cold I couldn't feel the sand beneath my fingers and toes. With my head straining to keep upright, all I could see was the instructor's boots as he walked around Marc and me.

"Once again you two officers have embarrassed your class." Another set of boots appeared in my view and then another. Several instructors were now surrounding us. "You have made all your team-mates look bad." He paused. "Recover, gentlemen!"

As Marc and I got to our feet we looked around the beach and suddenly realized we were the first swim pair to finish.

"You embarrassed them all right." The instructor smiled. "The second pair isn't even in sight."

Marc and I turned to look toward the ocean, and sure enough, there was no one in view.

"Well done, gentlemen. It looks like all that extra pain and suffering paid off." The instructor paused, stepped over, and shook our hands. "I'll be honored to serve with you when you get to the Teams."

We had made it. The long swim was the final tough event of training. Several days later Marc and I graduated.

Marc went on to have a distinguished career in the SEAL Teams and we remain close friends to this day.

In life you will face a lot of Circuses. You will pay for your failures. But, if you persevere, if you let those failures teach you and strengthen you, then you will be prepared to handle life's toughest moments.

―――

July 1983 was one of those tough moments. As I stood before the commanding officer, I thought my career as a Navy SEAL was over. I had just been relieved of my SEAL squadron, fired for trying to change the way my squadron was organized, trained, and conducted missions. There were some magnificent officers and enlisted men in the organization, some of the most professional warriors I had ever been around. However, much of the culture was still rooted in the Vietnam era, and I thought it was time for a change. As I was to find out, change is never easy, particularly for the person in charge.

Fortunately, even though I was fired, my commanding officer allowed me to transfer to another SEAL Team, but my reputation as a SEAL officer was severely damaged. Everywhere I went, other officers and enlisted men knew I had failed, and every day there were whispers and subtle reminders that maybe I wasn't up to the task of being a SEAL.

At that point in my career I had two options: quit and move on to civilian life, which seemed like the logical choice in light of my recent Officer Fitness Report, or weather the storm and prove to others and myself that I was a good SEAL officer. I chose the latter.

Soon after being fired, I was given a second chance, an opportunity to deploy overseas as the Officer in Charge of a SEAL platoon. Most of the time on that overseas deployment we were in remote locations, isolated and on our own. I took advantage of the opportunity to show that I could still lead. When you live in close quarters with twelve SEALs there isn't anywhere to hide. They know if you are giving 100 percent on the morning workout. They see when you are first in line to jump out of the airplane and last in line to get the chow. They watch you clean your weapon, check your radio, read the intelligence, and prepare your mission briefs. They know when you have worked all night preparing for tomorrow's training.

As month after month of the overseas deployment wore on, I used my previous failure as motivation to outwork, outhustle, and outperform everyone in the platoon. I sometimes fell short of being the best, but I never fell short of giving it my best.

In time, I regained the respect of my men. Several years later I was selected to command a SEAL Team of my own. Eventually I would go on to command all the SEALs on the West Coast.

By 2003, I found myself in combat in Iraq and Afghanistan. Now that I was a one-star admiral leading troops in a war zone, every decision I made had its consequences. Over the next several years, I stumbled often. But, for every failure, for every mistake, there were hundreds of successes: hostages rescued, suicide bombers stopped, pirates captured, terrorists killed, and countless lives saved.

I realized that the past failures had strengthened me, taught me that no one is immune from mistakes. True leaders must learn from their failures, use the lessons to motivate themselves, and not be afraid to try again or make the next tough decision.

You can't avoid The Circus. At some point we all make the list. Don't be afraid of The Circus.

CHAPTER SIX

You Must Dare Greatly

If you want to change the world . . .

slide down the obstacle headfirst.

S tanding at the edge of the thirty-foot tower, I grabbed the thick nylon rope. One end of the rope was attached to the tower and the other end anchored on the ground to a pole one hundred feet away. I was halfway through the SEAL obstacle course and I was on a record pace. Swinging my legs over the top of the line and holding on for dear life, I began to inch my way off the platform. My body hung underneath the rope, and with a caterpillar-like motion I slowly made my way, foot by foot, to the other end.

As I reached the end, I released my grip on the line, dropped into the soft sand, and ran to the next obstacle. The other students in my class were yelling encouragement, but I could hear the SEAL instructor calling out the minutes. I had lost a lot of time on the Slide for Life. My "possum-style" technique of negotiating the long rope was just too slow, but somehow I couldn't bring myself to slide down the rope headfirst. Going headfirst off the tower, using a method called Commando Style, was much faster but also much riskier. You were less stable on the top of the rope than hanging underneath, and if you fell and injured yourself, you would be washed out of the class.

I crossed the finish line with a disappointing time. As I was doubled over, trying to catch my breath, a grizzled old Vietnam vet with highly polished boots and a heavily starched green uniform stood hunched over me. "When are you going to learn, Mr. Mac?" he said with an unmistakable tone of contempt. "That obstacle course is going to beat you every time unless you start taking some risks."

One week later, I pushed my fears aside, mounted the top of the rope, and thrust my body headfirst down the Slide for Life. As I crossed the finish line in a personal best, I could see the old Vietnam SEAL nodding his approval. It was a simple lesson in overcoming your anxieties and trusting your abilities to get the job done. The lesson would serve me well in the years to come.

————

It was Iraq in 2004. The voice on the other end of the radio was calm but had an unmistakable sense of urgency. The three hostages we were searching for had been located. Al Qaeda terrorists were holding them in a walled compound on the outskirts of Baghdad. Unfortunately, intelligence indicated that terrorists were about to move the men, and we had to act quickly.

The Army lieutenant colonel in charge of the rescue mission informed me that they would have to conduct a dangerous daylight raid. To make matters worse, the only way to be successful was to land three Black Hawk helicopters, carrying the assault force, into the middle of the small compound. We talked through other tactical options, but it was clear the colonel was right. It was always preferable to conduct a rescue mission at night, when the element of surprise was on your side, but this was a fleeting opportunity, and if we didn't act now the hostages would be moved and possibly killed.

I approved the mission and within minutes the rescue force had boarded the three Black Hawk helicopters and was on its way to the compound. High above the Black Hawks, another helicopter was providing video surveillance back to my headquarters. I watched in silence as the three helicopters skimmed across the desert, just a few feet above the ground to hide their approach.

Inside the open courtyard, I could see one man, armed with an automatic weapon, moving in and out of the building, seemingly preparing to leave. The helos were five minutes out and all I could do from my headquarters was listen to the internal communications as the rescue force made final preparations.

This was not the first hostage rescue I had overseen, nor would it be the last, but it was clearly the most daring, in light of the need to gain surprise by landing inside the compound. While the pilots from the Army aviation unit were the best in the world, this was still a high-risk mission. Three helicopters, with blades extending beyond sixty feet, were going to land in a space with only inches to spare. Adding to the level of difficulty was an eight-foot-high brick wall that surrounded the compound, forcing the pilots to dramatically alter their approach angle. It was going to be a hard landing, and over the radio I could hear the rescue force preparing for impact.

From the overhead surveillance, I could see the helicopters' final approach. The first aircraft flew flat and level and then as it crossed over the wall the helo flared upward, settling into the tiny courtyard. Immediately the rescue force exited the Black Hawk and began surging into the building. The second helo, right on the tail of the first, landed within a few feet of his companion. Dirt from the downwash of the helicopters caused a cloud of dust to encircle the landing area. As the third helo approached the compound, a giant plume of dust temporarily blinded the pilot. The front of the third helo inched over the wall, but the rear wheel clipped the eight-foot-high barricade, throwing bricks everywhere. With no room to spare, the pilot forced the helo to the ground with a thud, but everyone inside was unharmed.

Minutes later, I received word that all the hostages were safe. Within thirty minutes the rescue force and the freed men were on their way back to safety. The gamble had paid off.

Over the course of the next decade I would come to realize that assuming risk was typical of our special operations forces. They always pushed the limits of themselves and their machines in order to be successful. In many ways this is what set them apart from everyone else. However, contrary to what outsiders saw, the risk was usually calculated, thoughtful, and well planned. Even if it was spontaneous, the operators knew their limits but believed in themselves enough to try.

Throughout my career, I always had great respect for the British Special Air Service, the famed SAS. The SAS motto was "Who Dares Wins." The motto was so widely admired that even moments before the bin Laden raid, my Command Sergeant Major, Chris Faris, quoted it to the SEALs preparing for the mission. To me the motto was more than about how the British special forces operated as a unit; it was about how each of us should approach our lives.

Life is a struggle and the potential for failure is ever present, but those who live in fear of failure, or hardship, or embarrassment will never achieve their potential. Without pushing your limits, without occasionally sliding down the rope headfirst, without daring greatly, you will never know what is truly possible in your life.

CHAPTER SEVEN

Stand Up to the Bullies

If you want to change the world . . .

don't back down from the sharks.

The water off San Clemente Island was choppy and cold as we began our four-mile night swim. Ensign Marc Thomas was matching my sidestrokes one for one. With nothing but a loose-fitting wet suit top, a mask, and a pair of fins, we swam hard against the current that was pushing southward around the small peninsula. The lights of the naval base from which we had started began to fade as we made our way out into the open ocean. Within an hour we were about a mile off the beach and seemingly all alone in the water. Whatever swimmers were around us were cloaked in darkness.

I could see Marc's eyes through the glass in his face mask. His expression must have mirrored mine. We both knew that the waters off San Clemente were filled with sharks. Not just any sharks, but great white sharks, the largest, most aggressive man-eater in the ocean. Prior to our swim, the SEAL instructors had given us a briefing on all the potential threats we might encounter that night. There were leopard sharks, mako sharks, hammerhead sharks, thresher sharks, but the one we feared the most was the great white.

There was something a little unnerving about being alone, at night, in the middle of the ocean, knowing that lurking beneath the surface was a prehistoric creature just waiting to bite you in half.

But we both wanted to be SEALs so badly that nothing in the water that night was going to stop us. If we had to fight off the sharks, then we were both prepared to do so. Our goal, which we believed to be honorable and noble, gave us courage, and courage is a remarkable quality. Nothing and nobody can stand in your way. Without it, others will define your path forward. Without it, you are at the mercy of life's temptations. Without courage, men will be ruled by tyrants and despots. Without courage, no great society can flourish. Without courage, the bullies of the world rise up. With it, you can accomplish any goal. With it, you can defy and defeat evil.

———

Saddam Hussein, the now former president of Iraq, sat on the edge of an old Army cot clad only in an orange jumpsuit. Having been captured by U.S. forces twenty-four hours earlier, he was now a prisoner of the United States.

As I opened the door to allow the new Iraqi government leaders into the room, Saddam remained seated. A smirk crossed his face, and there was no sign of remorse or submission in his attitude. Immediately, the four Iraqi leaders began to yell at Saddam, but from a safe distance. With a look of contempt, Saddam gave them a deadly smile and motioned them to sit down. Still fearful of the former dictator, they each grabbed a folding chair and took their seats. The screaming and finger-pointing continued but slowly subsided as the former dictator began to talk.

Under Saddam Hussein, the Baath Party was responsible for the deaths of thousands of Shia Iraqis and tens of thousands of Kurds. Saddam had personally executed a number of his own generals whom he felt were disloyal.

Although I was positive Saddam would no longer be a threat to the other men in the room, the Iraqi leaders were not so certain. The fear in their eyes was unmistakable. This man, the Butcher of Baghdad, had for decades terrorized an entire nation. His cult of personality had drawn to him followers of the worst sort. His murderous thugs had brutalized the innocent and forced thousands to flee the country. No one in Iraq had mustered the courage to challenge the tyrant. There was no doubt in my mind that these new leaders were still terrified of what Saddam might be able to do—even from behind bars.

If the purpose of the meeting was to show Saddam that he was no longer in power—it had failed. In those brief moments, Saddam had managed to intimidate and frighten the new regime leadership. He seemed more confident than ever.

As the Iraqi leaders left, I instructed my guards to isolate the former president in a small room. There would be no visitors, and the guards in the room were ordered not to talk with Saddam.

Over the next month, I visited the small room every day. And every day Saddam rose to greet me, and every day without speaking, I motioned him back to his cot. The message was clear. He was no longer important. He could no longer intimidate those around him. He could no longer instill fear into his subjects. Gone was the gleaming palace. Gone were the handmaidens, the servants, and the generals. Gone was the power. The arrogance and oppressiveness that had defined his rule had ended. Courageous young American soldiers had stood up to his tyranny, and now he was no longer a threat to anyone.

Thirty days later, I transferred Saddam Hussein to a proper military police unit, and a year later the Iraqis hanged him for his crimes against the nation.

Bullies are all the same; whether they are in the school yard, in the workplace, or ruling a country through terror. They thrive on fear and intimidation. Bullies gain their strength through the timid and faint of heart. They are like sharks that sense fear in the water. They will circle to see if their prey is struggling. They will probe to see if their victim is weak. If you don't find the courage to stand your ground, they will strike. In life, to achieve your goals, to complete the night swim, you will have to be men and women of great courage. That courage is within all of us. Dig deep, and you will find it in abundance.

CHAPTER EIGHT

Rise to the Occasion

If you want to change the world . . .

be your very best in the
darkest moments.

I stood on the small sandy spit of land, looking across the bay at the line of warships that were moored at 32nd Street Naval Base. In between the ships and our starting point was a small vessel anchored in San Diego Bay that would be this evening's "target." Our training class had spent the last several months learning to dive the basic SCUBA and the more advanced, bubbleless, Emerson closed-circuit diving rig. Tonight was the culmination of Dive Phase, the most technically difficult part of basic SEAL training.

Our objective was to swim the two thousand meters underwater from the starting point across the bay to the anchored vessel. Once underneath the ship, we were to place our practice limpet mine on the keel and then, without being detected, return to the beach. The Emerson diving apparatus was morbidly referred to as the "death rig." It was known to malfunction occasionally, and according to SEAL folklore a number of trainees had died over the years using the Emerson.

At night the visibility in San Diego Bay was so bad that you couldn't see your hand in front of your face. All you had was a small green chemical light to illuminate your underwater compass. To make matters worse the fog was rolling in. The haze hung low over the bay, making it difficult to take an initial compass bearing on our target. If you missed the target you would find yourself in the shipping channel, never a good place to be when a Navy destroyer was pulling into port.

The SEAL instructors paced back and forth in front of the twenty-five pairs of divers preparing for the night's dive. The instructors seemed as nervous as we were. They knew that this training event had the highest potential for someone to get hurt or die.

The chief petty officer in charge of the event summoned all the divers into a small circle. "Gentlemen," he said. "Tonight we find out which of you sailors really want to be frogmen." He paused for effect. "It's cold and dark out there. It will be darker under the ship. So dark that you can get disoriented. So dark that if you get separated from your swim buddy, he will not be able to find you." The fog was now closing in around us and the mist encircled even the spit of land on which we stood. "Tonight, you will have to be your very best. You must rise above your fears, your doubts, and your fatigue. No matter how dark it gets, you must complete the mission. This is what separates you from everyone else." Somehow those words stayed with me for the next thirty years.

———

As I watched the fog encircle the airfield at Bagram Air Base in Afghanistan, another dark moment was unfolding in front of me. A massive C-17 aircraft was parked on the tarmac, its ramp lowered, standing by to receive the remains of a fallen warrior.

This was a Ramp Ceremony. It was one of the

most solemn and yet unquestionably inspiring aspects of the wars in Iraq and Afghanistan. It was America at its finest. Every man, every woman, regardless of their background, regardless of how heroic their final moments, was treated with incredible dignity and honor. It was our nation's way of recognizing their sacrifice. It was our last salute, our final thanks, and a prayer to send them on their way home.

Extending out from the ramp were two parallel lines of soldiers. Standing at parade rest, they formed the honor guard. Off to the right of the airplane was a small three-piece band softly playing "Amazing Grace."

A few others, myself included, were gathered to the left, and all along hangar row stood hundreds of other soldiers, sailors, airmen, Marines, civilians, and our allies. They had all come to pay their last respects.

The HUMVEE tactical vehicle carrying the remains arrived right on time. Six men from the fallen heroes unit acted as pallbearers. Off-loading the flag-draped casket, they slowly marched through the honor guard, up the ramp, and onto the plane.

They positioned the casket in the middle of the cargo bay, turned smartly, came to attention, and saluted. At the head of the casket, the pastor bowed his head and read from Isaiah 6:8.

"And I heard the voice of the Lord saying, Whom shall I send and who will go for us? And I said, Here I am. Send me!"

As "Taps" was played, tears rolled down the soldiers' faces. There was no attempt to hide their pain.

As the pallbearers departed, those lined up outside came through one by one, saluting, and kneeling by the casket for one last thought.

The C-17 would depart later that morning, refueling along the way and arriving at Dover Air Force Base. There, another honor guard, along with the family of the fallen soldier, would meet the casket and escort it home.

There is no darker moment in life than losing

someone you love, and yet I watched time and again as families, as military units, as towns, as cities, and as a nation, how we came together to be our best during those tragic times.

When a seasoned Army special operator was killed in Iraq, his twin brother stood tall, comforting the soldier's friends, holding the family together, and ensuring that his lost brother would be proud of his strength in this time of need.

When a fallen Ranger was returned home to his base in Savannah, Georgia, his entire unit, dressed in their finest uniforms, marched from the church to the Ranger's favorite bar on River Street. All along the route, the town of Savannah turned out. Firefighters, police officers, veterans, civilians from all walks of life, were there to salute the young soldier who had died heroically in Afghanistan.

When a CV-22 aircraft crashed in Afghanistan, killing the pilot and several crewmen, the airmen from the same unit came together, paid their respects, and flew the next day—knowing that their fallen brothers would want them in the air, continuing the mission.

When a helicopter crash took the lives of twenty-five special operators and six National Guard soldiers, the entire nation mourned but also took incredible pride in the courage, patriotism, and valor of the fallen warriors.

At some point we will all confront a dark moment in life. If not the passing of a loved one, then something else that crushes your spirit and leaves you wondering about your future. In that dark moment, reach deep inside yourself and be your very best.

CHAPTER NINE

Give People Hope

If you want to change the world . . .

start singing when you're up to your neck in mud.

♫

The night wind coming off the ocean was gusting to twenty miles an hour. There was no moon out, and an evening layer of low clouds obscured the stars. I was sitting in chest-deep mud, covered from head to toe with a layer of grime. My vision blurred by the caked-on clay, I could see only the outline of my fellow students lined up in the pit beside me.

It was Wednesday of Hell Week, and my SEAL training class was down at the infamous Tijuana mudflats. Hell Week was the seminal event for the First Phase of SEAL training. It was six days of no sleep and unrelenting harassment by the instructors. There were long runs, open ocean swims, obstacle courses, rope climbs, endless sessions of calisthenics, and constant paddling of the inflatable boat small (IBS). The purpose of Hell Week was to eliminate the weak, those not tough enough to be SEALs.

Statistically speaking, more students quit during Hell Week than at any other time in training, and the mudflats were the toughest part of the week. Located between South San Diego and Mexico, the mudflats were a low-lying area where drainage from San Diego created a large swath of deep, thick mud that had the consistency of wet clay.

Earlier that afternoon, our class had paddled our rubber boats from Coronado down to the mudflats. Soon after arriving we were ordered into the mud and began a series of races and individual competitions designed to keep us cold, wet, and miserable. The mud clung to every part of your body. It was so dense that moving through it exhausted you and tested your will to carry on.

For hours the races continued. By the evening, we could barely move from the bone-chilling coldness and the fatigue. As the sun went down the temperature dropped, the wind picked up, and everything seemed to get even harder.

Morale was declining rapidly. It was only Wednesday, and we all knew that another three days of pain and exhaustion lay ahead. This was the moment of truth for a lot of the students. Shaking uncontrollably, with hands and feet swollen from nonstop use and skin so tender that even the slightest movement brought discomfort, our hope for completing the training was fading fast.

Silhouetted against the distant lights of the city, a SEAL instructor walked purposefully to the edge of the mudflats. Sounding like an old friend, he softly talked into a bullhorn and offered comfort to the suffering trainees. We could join him and the other instructors by the fire, he said. He had hot coffee and chicken soup. We could relax until the sun came up. Get off our feet. Take it easy.

I could sense that some of the students were ready to accept his offer. After all, how much longer could we survive in the mud? A warm fire, hot coffee, and chicken soup sure sounded good. But then came the catch. All he needed was for five of us to quit. Just five quitters and the rest of the class could have some relief from the pain.

The student beside me started to move toward the instructor. I grabbed his arm and held him tight, but the urge to leave the mud was too great. He broke free of my grasp and began to lunge for dry ground. I could see the instructor smiling. He knew that once one man quit, others would follow.

Suddenly, above the howl of the wind came a voice. Singing. It was tired and raspy, but loud enough to be heard by all. The lyrics were not meant for tender ears, but everyone knew the tune. One voice became two and two became three and then before long everyone was singing.

The student rushing for the dry ground turned around and came back beside me. Looping his arm around mine, he began to sing as well. The instructor grabbed the bullhorn and shouted for the class to quit singing. No one did. He yelled at the class leader to get control of the trainees. The singing continued. With each threat from the instructor, the voices got louder, the class got stronger, and the will to continue on in the face of adversity became unbreakable. In the darkness, with the fire reflecting on the face of the instructor, I could see him smile. Once again, we had learned an important lesson: the power of one person to unite the group, the power of one person to inspire those around him, to give them hope. If that one person could sing while neck deep in mud, then so could we. If that one person could endure the freezing cold, then so could we. If that one person could hold on, then so could we.

———

The large room at Dover Air Force Base was filled with grieving families—inconsolable children sobbing in their mothers' arms, parents holding hands hoping to gain strength from each other, and wives with a far-off look of disbelief. Just five days earlier, a helicopter carrying Navy SEALs and their Afghan Special Operations partners, and flown by Army aviators had been shot down in Afghanistan. All thirty-eight men on board were killed. It was the single greatest loss in the War on Terror.

In less than an hour, a large C-17 transport aircraft was scheduled to land at Dover, and the families of the fallen heroes would be escorted to the flight line to meet the flag-draped coffins. But as the families waited, the President of the United States, the Secretary of Defense, the service secretaries, and senior military leaders filed into the waiting room to pay their respects and give comfort where they could.

I had attended dozens of services for fallen soldiers. It was never easy, and I often wondered whether my words of solace made any difference to those who lost loved ones or whether the shock of their loss made everything I said incomprehensible.

As my wife, Georgeann, and I began to talk with the families I struggled with the right words.

How could I truly empathize with their pain? How could I tell them that the sacrifice of their son, their husband, their father, their brother, their friend, was worth it? I did my best to console each one. I hugged them. I prayed with them. I tried to remain strong for them, but somehow I knew my words fell short.

Then, as I knelt down beside an elderly woman, I noticed the family next to me talking with Marine Lieutenant General John Kelly. The military assistant to the Secretary of Defense, Kelly was tall, lean, with close-cropped gray hair and dressed in an immaculate Marine uniform. The family was gathered around him, and I could sense that his words of sympathy and encouragement in the face of this tragedy were having a profound effect on the grief-stricken parents and their children. He smiled and they smiled. He hugged and they hugged back. He reached out his hand and they grasped it tightly.

After embracing the parents one last time and thanking the family for their sacrifice, Kelly moved on to the next group of heartbroken survivors. During the next hour, John Kelly touched almost every family in the room. More than any other visitor that day Kelly's words resonated with every parent, every wife, every brother and sister, and every friend. His words were words of understanding. His were words of compassion, and above all, his were words of hope.

Only John Kelly could have made a difference that day. Only John Kelly could have given them hope, because only John Kelly knew what it was like to lose a son in combat.

Marine First Lieutenant Robert Kelly was killed in Afghanistan in 2010 while serving with the Third Battalion, Fifth Marines. General Kelly and his family had struggled with the tragedy, just like the families at Dover that day. But the Kelly family had survived. They had endured through the pain, the heartache, and the inconsolable sense of loss.

As I watched him that day he also gave me strength. The truth is, when you lose a soldier you grieve for the families, but you also fear that the same fate may someday befall you. You wonder whether you could survive the loss of a child. Or you wonder how your family would get along without you by their side. You hope and pray that God will be merciful and not have you shoulder this unthinkable burden.

Over the course of the next three years, John Kelly and I became close friends. He was a remarkable officer, a strong husband to his wife, Karen, and a loving father to his daughter, Kate, and oldest son, Marine Major John Kelly. But more than that, without ever knowing it, John Kelly gave all those around him hope. Hope that in the very worst of times we could rise above the pain, the disappointment, and the agony and be strong. That we each had within us the ability to carry on and not only to survive but also to inspire others.

Hope is the most powerful force in the universe. With hope you can inspire nations to greatness. With hope you can raise up the downtrodden.

With hope you can ease the pain of unbearable loss. Sometimes all it takes is one person to make a difference.

We will all find ourselves neck deep in mud someday. That is the time to sing loudly, to smile broadly, to lift up those around you and give them hope that tomorrow will be a better day.

CHAPTER TEN

Never, Ever Quit!

If you want to change the world . . .

don't ever, ever ring the bell.

I stood at attention along with the other 150 students beginning the first day of SEAL training. The instructor, dressed in combat boots, khaki shorts, and a blue and gold tee shirt, walked across the large asphalt courtyard to a brass bell hanging in full view of all the trainees.

"Gentlemen," he began. "Today is the first day of SEAL training. For the next six months you will undergo the toughest course of instruction in the United States military."

I glanced around and could see some looks of apprehension on the faces of my fellow students.

The instructor continued. "You will be tested like no time in your life." Pausing, he looked around the class of new "tadpoles." "Most of you will not make it through. I will see to that." He smiled. "I will do everything in my power to make you quit!" He emphasized the last three words. "I will harass you unmercifully. I will embarrass you in front of your teammates. I will push you beyond your limits." Then a slight grin crossed his face. "And there will be pain. Lots and lots of pain."

Grabbing the bell, he pulled the rope hard and a loud clanging noise echoed across the courtyard. "But if you don't like the pain, if you don't like all the harassment, then there is an easy way out." He pulled the rope again and another wave of deep metallic sound reverberated off the buildings. "All you have to do to quit is ring this bell three times."

He let go of the rope tied to the bell's clapper. "Ring the bell and you won't have to get up early. Ring the bell and you won't have to do the long runs, the cold swims, or the obstacle course. Ring the bell and you can avoid all this pain."

Then the instructor glanced down at the asphalt and seemed to break from his prepared monologue. "But let me tell you something," he said. "If you quit, you will regret it for the rest of your life. Quitting never makes anything easier."

Six months later, there were only thirty-three of us standing at graduation. Some had taken the easy way out. They had quit, and my guess is the instructor was right, they would regret it for the rest of their lives.

Of all the lessons I learned in SEAL training, this was the most important. Never quit. It doesn't sound particularly profound, but life constantly puts you in situations where quitting seems so much easier than continuing on. Where the odds are so stacked against you that giving up seems the rational thing to do.

Throughout my career, I was constantly inspired by men and women who refused to quit, who refused to feel sorry for themselves, but none more so than a young Army Ranger I met in a hospital in Afghanistan.

———

It was late one evening when I received word that one of my soldiers had stepped on a pressure plate mine and had been MEDEVACed to the combat hospital near my headquarters. The Ranger regimental commander, Colonel Erik Kurilla, and I quickly made our way to the hospital and into the soldier's room.

The soldier lay in the hospital bed, tubes extending from his mouth and chest; blast burns streaked up his arms and across his face. The blanket covering his body lay flat to the bed where his legs would normally have been. His life was now changed forever.

I had made countless visits to the combat hospital in Afghanistan. As a wartime leader you try not to internalize the human suffering. You know that it is part of combat. Soldiers get wounded. Soldiers die. If you allow every decision you make to be predicated on the possible loss of life you will struggle mightily to be effective.

Somehow though this night seemed different. The Ranger lying in front of me was so very young: younger than my two boys. He was nineteen years old and his name was Adam Bates. He had arrived in Afghanistan just a week earlier and this had been his first combat mission. I leaned over and touched my hand to his shoulder. He appeared to be sedated and unconscious. I reflected for a minute, said a little prayer, and was starting to leave when the nurse came in to check on my soldier.

She smiled, looked at his vitals, and asked me if I had any questions regarding his status. She informed me that both of his legs had been amputated and that he had serious blast injuries, but that his chance for survival was good.

I thanked her for taking such great care of Ranger Bates and told her I would return when he was conscious. "Oh, he's conscious," she stated. "In fact it would be good for you to talk with him." She gently shook the young Ranger, who opened his eyes slightly and acknowledged my presence.

"He can't speak right now," the nurse said. "But his mother was deaf and he knows how to sign." The nurse handed me a sheet of paper with the various sign language symbols displayed on it.

I talked for a minute, trying to find the strength

to say the right thing. What do you tell a young man who has lost both his legs serving his country? How do you make him feel better about his future?

Bates, his face swollen from the blast, his eyes barely visible through the redness and the bandages, stared at me momentarily. He must have sensed the pity in my expression.

Raising his hand, he began to sign.

I looked at each symbol on the sheet of paper before me. Slowly, painfully, he signed, "I—will—be—OK." And then he fell back asleep.

As I left the hospital that evening I could not help but cry. Of the hundreds of men I talked with in the hospital, never once did anyone complain. Never once! They were proud of their service. They were accepting of their fate, and all they wanted was to get back to their unit, to be with the men that they had left behind. Somehow Adam Bates personified all those men who had come before him.

A year after my hospital visit in Afghanistan, I was at the Seventy-fifth Ranger Regimental Change of Command. There in the stands was Ranger Bates, looking sharp in his dress uniform and standing tall on his new prosthetic legs. I overheard him challenge a number of his fellow Rangers to a pull-up contest. With all he had been through—the multiple surgeries, the painful rehab, and adjusting to a new life—he never quit. He was laughing, joking, smiling—and just as he promised me—he was okay!

Life is full of difficult times. But someone out there always has it worse than you do. If you fill your days with pity, sorrowful for the way you have been treated, bemoaning your lot in life, blaming your circumstances on someone or something else, then life will be long and hard. If, on the other hand, you refuse to give up on your dreams, stand tall and strong against the odds—then life will be what you make of it—and you can make it great. Never, ever, ring the bell!

———

Remember...start each day with a task completed. Find someone to help you through life. Respect everyone. Know that life is not fair and that you will fail often. But if you take some risks, step up when times are toughest, face down the bullies, lift up the downtrodden, and never, ever give up—if you do these things, then you can change your life for the better... and maybe the world!

THE UNIVERSITY OF TEXAS
COMMENCEMENT SPEECH

May 17, 2014

The University's slogan is "What starts here changes the world." I have to admit, I kind of like it. "What starts here changes the world!"

Tonight there are almost eight thousand students graduating from the University of Texas. That great paragon of analytical rigor, Ask.com, says that the average American will meet ten thousand people in their lifetime. That's a lot of folks. But, if every one of you changed the lives of just ten people, and each one of those folks changed the lives of another ten people—just ten—then in five generations—125 years—the class of 2014 will have changed the lives of 800 million people.

Eight hundred million people. Think of it: over twice the population of the United States. Go one more generation and you can change the entire population of the world, eight billion people. If you think it's hard to change the lives of ten people, change their lives forever, you're wrong.

I saw it happen every day in Iraq and Afghanistan. A young Army officer makes a decision to go left instead of right down a road in Baghdad and the ten soldiers in his squad are saved from a close-in ambush.

In Kandahar province, Afghanistan, a non-commissioned officer from the Female Engagement Team senses something isn't right and directs the infantry platoon away from a five-hundred-pound IED, saving the lives of a dozen soldiers.

But, if you think about it, not only were these soldiers saved by the decisions of one person, but their children yet unborn were also saved. And their children's children were saved. Generations were saved by one decision, by one person.

But changing the world can happen anywhere, and anyone can do it. So, what starts here can indeed change the world, but the question is: What will the world look like after you change it?

Well, I am confident that it will look much, much better, but if you will humor this old sailor for just a moment, I have a few suggestions that may help you on your way to a better world. And while these lessons were learned during my time in the military, I can assure you that it matters not whether you ever served a day in uniform.

It matters not your gender, your ethnic or religious background, your orientation, or your social status. Our struggles in this world are similar and the lessons to overcome those struggles and to move forward—changing ourselves and the world around us—will apply equally to all.

I have been a Navy SEAL for thirty-six years. But it all began when I left UT for basic SEAL training in Coronado, California. Basic SEAL training is six months of long torturous runs in the soft sand, midnight swims in the cold water off San Diego, obstacle courses, unending calisthenics, days without sleep, and always being cold, wet, and miserable.

It is six months of being constantly harassed by professionally trained warriors who seek to find the weak of mind and body and eliminate them from ever becoming a Navy SEAL. But the training also seeks to find those students who can lead in an environment of constant stress, chaos, failure, and hardships. To me, basic SEAL training was a lifetime of challenges crammed into six months.

So, here are the ten lessons I learned from basic SEAL training that hopefully will be of value to you as you move forward in life.

———

Every morning in basic SEAL training, my instructors, who at the time were all Vietnam veterans, would show up in my barracks room, and the first thing they would inspect was your bed. If you did it right, the corners would be square, the covers pulled tight, the pillow centered just under the headboard, and the extra blanket folded neatly at the foot of the rack.

It was a simple task, mundane at best. But every morning we were required to make our bed to perfection. It seemed a little ridiculous at the time, particularly in light of the fact that we were aspiring to be real warriors, tough battle-hardened SEALs, but the wisdom of this simple act has been proven to me many times over.

If you make your bed every morning, you will have accomplished the first task of the day. It will give you a small sense of pride and it will encourage you to do another task and another and another. By the end of the day, that one task completed will have turned into many tasks completed. Making your bed will also reinforce the fact that little things in life matter.

If you can't do the little things right, you will never do the big things right. And, if by chance you have a miserable day, you will come home to a bed that is made—that you made—and a made bed gives you encouragement that tomorrow will be better.

If you want to change the world, start off by making your bed.

———

During SEAL training the students are broken down into boat crews. Each crew is seven students: three on each side of a small rubber boat and one coxswain to help guide the dinghy. Every day your boat crew forms up on the beach and is instructed to get through the surf zone and paddle several miles down the coast.

In the winter, the surf off San Diego can get to be eight to ten feet high and it is exceedingly difficult to paddle through the plunging surf unless everyone digs in. Every paddle must be synchronized to the stroke count of the coxswain. Everyone must exert equal effort or the boat will turn against the wave and be unceremoniously tossed back on the beach.

For the boat to make it to its destination, everyone must paddle.

You can't change the world alone—you will need some help—and to truly get from your starting point to your destination takes friends, colleagues, the goodwill of strangers, and a strong coxswain to guide them.

If you want to change the world, find someone to help you paddle.

———

Over a few weeks of difficult training, my SEAL class, which started with 150 men, was down to just 42. There were now 6 boat crews of 7 men each. I was in the boat with the tall guys, but the best boat crew we had was made up of the little guys—"the munchkin crew," we called them. No one was over about five foot five.

The munchkin boat crew had one American Indian, one African American, one Polish American, one Greek American, one Italian American, and two tough kids from the Midwest. They outpaddled, outran, and outswam all the other boat crews.

The big men in the other boat crews would always make good-natured fun of the *tiny little flippers* the munchkins put on their *tiny little feet* prior to every swim. But somehow these little guys, from every corner of the nation and the world, always had the last laugh, swimming faster than everyone and reaching the shore long before the rest of us.

SEAL training was a great equalizer. Nothing mattered but your will to succeed; not your color, not your ethnic background, not your education, and not your social status.

If you want to change the world, measure a person by the size of their heart, not the size of their flippers.

———

Several times a week, the instructors would line up the class and do a uniform inspection. It was exceptionally thorough. Your hat had to be perfectly starched, your uniform immaculately pressed, and your belt buckle shiny and devoid of any smudges.

But it seemed that no matter how much effort you put into starching your hat or pressing your uniform or polishing your belt buckle, it just wasn't good enough. The instructors would find "something" wrong.

For failing the uniform inspection, the student had to run, fully clothed, into the surf zone and then, wet from head to toe, roll around on the beach until every part of his body was covered with sand. The effect was known as a "sugar cookie." You stayed in that uniform the rest of the day, cold, wet, and sandy.

There were many students who just couldn't accept the fact that all their effort was in vain. That no matter how hard they tried to get the uniform right, it was unappreciated. Those students didn't make it through training. Those students didn't understand the purpose of the drill. You were never going to succeed. You were never going to have a perfect uniform.

Sometimes no matter how well you prepare or how well you perform you still end up as a sugar cookie. It's just the way life is sometimes.

If you want to change the world, get over being a sugar cookie and keep moving forward.

———

Every day during training you were challenged with multiple physical events. Long runs, long swims, obstacle courses, and hours of calisthenics, something designed to test your mettle.

Every event had standards: times you had to meet. If you failed to meet those standards your name was posted on a list, and at the end of the day those on the list were invited to a Circus.

A Circus was two hours of additional calisthenics designed to wear you down, to break your spirit, to force you to quit. No one wanted a circus. A Circus meant that, for that day, you didn't measure up. A Circus meant more fatigue, and more fatigue meant that the following day would be more difficult—and more Circuses were likely.

But at some time during SEAL training, everyone—everyone—made the Circus list. And an interesting thing happened to those who were constantly on the list. Over time those students, who did two hours of extra calisthenics, got stronger and stronger. The pain of the Circuses built inner strength, built physical resiliency.

Life is filled with circuses. You will fail. You will likely fail often. It will be painful. It will be discouraging. At times it will test you to your very core.

If you want to change the world, don't be afraid of the Circuses.

———

At least twice a week, the trainees were required to run the obstacle course. The obstacle course contained twenty-five obstacles including a ten-foot-high wall, a thirty-foot cargo net, and a barbed-wire crawl, to name a few.

But the most challenging obstacle was the "Slide for Life." It had a three-level, thirty-foot tower at one end and a one-level tower at the other. In between was a hundred-foot-long rope.

You had to climb the three-tiered tower and, once at the top, you grabbed the rope, swung underneath the rope, and pulled yourself hand over hand until you got to the other end. The record for the obstacle course had stood for years when my class began training in 1977. The record seemed unbeatable, until one day, a student decided to go down the Slide for Life—headfirst.

Instead of swinging his body underneath the rope and inching his way down, he bravely mounted the top of the rope and thrust himself forward. It was a dangerous move, seemingly foolish, and fraught with risk. Failure could mean injury and being dropped from the training. Without hesitation, the student slid down the rope perilously fast, and instead of several minutes, it took him only half that time. By the end of the course he had broken the record.

If you want to change the world, sometimes you have to slide down the obstacle headfirst.

———

During the land warfare phase of training, the students are flown out to San Clemente Island, which lies off the coast of San Diego. The waters off San Clemente are a breeding ground for great white sharks. To pass SEAL training there are a series of long swims that must be completed. One is the night swim.

Before the swim the instructors joyfully brief the trainees on all the species of sharks that inhabit the waters off San Clemente. They assure you, however, that no student has ever been eaten by a shark—at least not recently.

But you are also taught that if a shark begins to circle your position—stand your ground. Do not swim away. Do not act afraid. And if the shark, hungry for a midnight snack, darts toward you—then summon up all your strength and punch him in the snout, and he will turn and swim away.

There are a lot of sharks in the world. If you hope to complete the swim you will have to deal with them.

If you want to change the world, don't back down from the sharks.

———

One of our jobs as Navy SEALs is to conduct underwater attacks against enemy shipping. We practiced this technique extensively during basic training. The ship attack mission is where a pair of SEAL divers is dropped off outside an enemy harbor and then they swim well over two miles underwater using nothing but a depth gauge and a compass to get to their target.

During the entire swim, even well below the surface there is some light that comes through. It is comforting to know that there is open water above you. But as you approach the ship, which is tied to a pier, the light begins to fade. The steel structure of the ship blocks the moonlight; it blocks the surrounding street lamps. It blocks all ambient light.

To be successful in your mission, you have to swim under the ship and find the keel, the center line and the deepest part of the ship. This is your objective. But the keel is also the darkest part of the ship, where you cannot see your hand in front of your face, where the noise from the ship's machinery is deafening, and where it is easy to get disoriented and fail.

Every SEAL knows that under the keel, at the darkest moment of the mission, is the time when you must be calm—composed—when all your tactical skills, your physical power, and all your inner strength must be brought to bear.

If you want to change the world, you must be your very best in the darkest moment.

———

The ninth week of training is referred to as Hell Week. It is six days of no sleep, constant physical and mental harassment, and one special day at the mudflats. The mudflats are an area between San Diego and Tijuana where the water runs off and creates the Tijuana slues, a swampy patch of terrain where the mud will engulf you.

It is on Wednesday of Hell Week that you paddle down to the mudflats and spend the next fifteen hours trying to survive the freezing cold mud, the howling wind, and the incessant pressure from the instructors to quit.

As the sun began to set that Wednesday evening, my training class, having committed some "egregious infraction of the rules," was ordered into the mud. The mud consumed each man till there was nothing visible but our heads. The instructors told us we could leave the mud if only five men would quit; just five men and we could get out of the oppressive cold.

As I looked around the mudflats, it was apparent that some students were about to give up. It was still over eight hours till the sun came up, eight more hours of bone-chilling cold. The chattering teeth and shivering moans of the trainees were so loud it was hard to hear anything. And then, one voice began to echo through the night, one voice raised in song. The song was terribly out of tune, but sung with great enthusiasm. One voice became two and two became three and before long everyone in the class was singing.

We knew that if one man could rise above the misery, then others could as well. The instructors threatened us with more time in the mud if we kept up the singing, but the singing persisted. And somehow the mud seemed a little warmer, the wind a little tamer, and the dawn not so far away.

If I have learned anything in my time traveling the world, it is the power of hope. The power of one person, a Washington, Lincoln, King, Mandela, and even a young girl from Pakistan, Malala. One person can change the world by giving people hope.

If you want to change the world, start singing when you're up to your neck in mud.

———

Finally, in SEAL training there is a bell, a brass bell that hangs in the center of the compound for all the students to see. All you have to do to quit is ring the bell. Ring the bell and you no longer have to wake up at five o'clock. Ring the bell and you no longer have to do the freezing cold swims. Ring the bell and you no longer have to do the runs, the obstacle course, the PT, and you no longer have to endure the hardships of training.

Just ring the bell.

If you want to change the world, don't ever, ever ring the bell.

———

To the graduating class of 2014, you are moments away from graduating. Moments away from beginning your journey through life. Moments away from starting to change the world, for the better. It will not be easy.

Start each day with a task completed. Find someone to help you through life. Respect everyone.

Know that life is not fair and that you will fail often, but if you take some risks, step up when the times are toughest, face down the bullies, lift up the downtrodden, and never, ever give up...if you do these things, then the next generation and the generations that follow will live in a world far better than the one we have today. And what started here will indeed have changed the world, for the better.

Thank you very much. Hook 'em, Horns.

ACKNOWLEDGMENTS

I would like to thank my editor Jamie Raab for her patience and understanding. You crafted a beautiful book that I know will stand the test of time. I also want to thank all those great friends who agreed to be mentioned in the book. Your courage in the face of tremendous adversity inspired me more than you will ever know.

ABOUT THE AUTHOR

Admiral William H. McRaven (U.S. Navy retired) served with great distinction in the Navy. In his thirty-seven years as a Navy SEAL, he commanded at every level. As a Four-Star Admiral, his final assignment was as Commander of all U.S. Special Operations Forces. He is now Chancellor of the University of Texas System.